I CAN PLAY SPORTS!

Snowboarding

by Thomas Kingsley Troupe

Kaleidoscope
Minneapolis, MN

Where the Quest for Discovery Begins

This edition first published in 2023 by Kaleidoscope Publishing, Inc.

For information regarding permission, write to

Kaleidoscope Publishing, Inc.
6012 Blue Circle Drive
Minnetonka, MN 55343

Library of Congress Control Number
2022937560

ISBN
978-1-64519-586-3 (library bound)
978-1-64519-656-3 (ebook)

Bigfoot Jr. lurks within one of the images in this book. It's up to you to find him!

Table of Contents

Downhill

The **snowboarder** buckles into their board. It's time to shred some snow! They slide down the hill.

The snowboard moves faster. The boarder jumps and spins in the air. I can snowboard!

Snowboarding is a winter sport. Snowboards only work on hills covered with snow.

Some snowboard hills have ramps or jumps. They are there for snowboarders to do tricks and **stunts**.

Boarders should wear warm clothes and gloves. A coat and snow pants can keep them warm.

Wearing a helmet is a good idea too. **Goggles** will keep snow out of the boarder's eyes.

FUN FACT
Sherman Poppen invented the snowboard in Muskegon, Michigan, in 1965.

Meet the Boarder

Snowboarding is a **solo** sport. Boarders try tricks and stunts on their snowboard.

Some snowboarders race down the hill. They are timed to see how fast they reach the end.

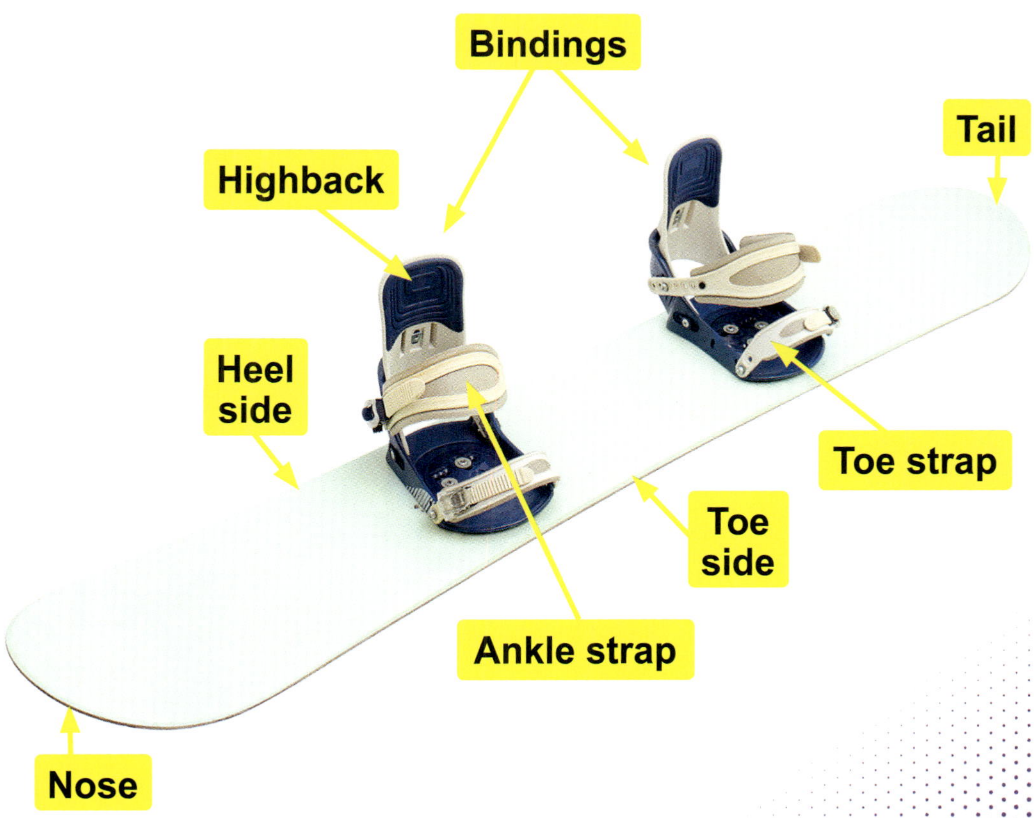

Snowboarding takes practice. It can be hard to stay standing up on a snowboard.

A snowboarder's feet are stuck to the board. When they move, the board moves with them!

FUN FACT
The highest anyone ever jumped on a snowboard was 32.2 feet (9.8 meters)!

Fresh Powder

Snowboard stunts are done on a half-pipe. The hills on each side help build up speed.

In the air, a snowboarder can flip or spin. Sometimes they will grab their board.

FUN FACT

Shaun White became a professional snowboarder at age 13.

There are five basic skills in snowboarding

1 Standing
getting up to stand on a snowboard

2 Stopping
coming to a stop on a snowboard

3 Balance
staying on the board without tipping over

4 Turning
using the board to turn left or right

5 Leafing
moving back and forth down the hill

A rail trick is sliding a snowboard on a rail. Boarders can turn their boards as they slide.

Spins in the air are called **rotations**. The more spins, the better the trick!

Front Flip!

Some snowboarders will **compete** against other boarders. They perform tricks or race down the hill.

Judges award points for stunts and fast racing times. Boarders lose points for falling down or going too slow.

FUN FACT

Snowboarding was added to the Olympic Games in 1998.

Boarders get three tries to do their best run. The judges use the best score for each snowboarder.

At the end of the day, the event is over. The boarders had fun. Let's try snowboarding again!

Photo Glossary

compete: When people take part in a game or contest.

goggles: Eyewear that is worn to protect a boarder's eyes.

judges: A group of people who score sporting events.

rotations: The spins a boarder does high in the air.

snowboarder: A person who rides on a snowboard.

solo: When a person does something alone, by themselves.

stunts: The tricks boarders do to get attention and have fun.

Read More

Abdo, Kenny. *Snowboarding.* Mankato, MN, ABDO Publishing, 2017.

Latchana Kenney, Karen. *Extreme Snowboarding Challenges.* Minneapolis, MN, Lerner Publishing, 2021.

McClellan, Ray. *Snowboarding.* Hopkins, MN, Bellwether Media, 2010.

Factsurfer.com gives you a safe, fun way to find more information.

1. Go to www.factsurfer.com.
2. Enter "Snowboarding" into the search box and click 🔍
3. Select your book cover to see a list of related websites.

About the Author

Thomas Kingsley Troupe has been reading and writing stories from a very young age. He's the author of over 100 books for kids of all ages. When he's not putting words together, he's fixing his house, watching movies, ghost-hunting or thinking about taking a nap. Thomas lives in Woodbury, MN, with his two ridiculous sons.

INDEX

PHOTO CREDITS

The images in this book are reproduced through the courtesy of: Sergiy Bykhunenko/Shutterstock Images, cover (top); Sergey Novikov/Shutterstock Images, cover (top right); Artur Didyk/Shutterstock Images,cover, 1 (bottom); Mikhail Valeev/Shutterstock Images, p. 3; Herrndorff image/Shutterstock Images, p. 4–5; Dmytro Vietrov/Shutterstock Images, p. 5; Lilkin/Shutterstock Images, p. 6–7; Oleksandr Rzhanitsyn/Shutterstock Images, p. 8; Ruslan Kalnitsky/Shutterstock Images, p. 9; BomMostFor/Shutterstock Images, p. 9, 22 (goggles); Dmytro Vietrov/Shutterstock Images, p. 10; ninikas/Shutterstock Images, p. 11; Izf/Shutterstock Images, p. 12; Yulia Raneva/Shutterstock Images, p. 13; Brandon Hirt/Shutterstock Images, p. 14; COLOMBO NICOLA/Shutterstock Images, p. 14 (circle); Artur Didyk/Shutterstock Images, p. 15; s_bukley/Shutterstock Images, p. 15 (Fun Fact); yanik88/Shutterstock Images, p. 16 (standing); UfaBizPhoto/Shutterstock Images, p. 16 (stopping); SandraMC/Shutterstock Images, p. 16 (balance); bullet74/Shutterstock Images, p. 16 (turning); SERGEI BRIK/Shutterstock Images, p. 16 (leafing); Andrew Angelov/Shutterstock Images, p. 17 (top); Flystock/Shutterstock Images, p. 17; masik0553/Shutterstock Images, p. 18–19; nyker/Shutterstock Images, p. 19 (Fun Fact); robinmacdonald/Shutterstock Images, p.20; Andrew Angelov/Shutterstock Images, p. 21 (top); s-ts/Shutterstock Images, p. 21; Suzanne Tucker/Shutterstock Images, p. 22 (compete); Andrey_Popov/Shutterstock Images, p. 22 (judges); Flystock/Shutterstock Images, p. 22 (rotations); Maxim Blinkov/Shutterstock Images, p. 22 (snowboarder); Michaela Jurasova/Shutterstock Images, p. 22 (solo); Herrndorff image/Shutterstock Images, p. 22 (stunts); Lilkin/Shutterstock Images, p. 23.